D1505740

SONGS · FOR SURVIVAL

SONGS · FOR SURVIVAL

SONGS AND CHANTS FROM TRIBAL PEOPLES AROUND THE WORLD

COMPILED BY

NIKKI SIEGEN-SMITH

ILLUSTRATED BY

BERNARD LODGE

DUTTON CHILDREN'S BOOKS ◆ NEW YORK

Frieze copyright © Cica Fitipaldi, Commission for the Creation of the Yanomami Park, Brazil

CIP Data is available.

Published in the United States 1996 by Dutton Children's Books,
a division of Penguin Books USA Inc.
375 Hudson Street, New York, New York 10014

Originally published in Great Britain 1995 by Barefoot Books Ltd,
Bristol, England.

Jacket design and display typography by Amy Berniker
Printed in Singapore   First American Edition
1 3 5 7 9 10 8 6 4 2
ISBN 0-525-45564-7

CONTENTS

INTRODUCTION

Can you imagine a birthday party without people singing "Happy Birthday"? How can there be any festival without its own special songs? Long ago, our ancestors sang songs to commemorate all kinds of events in their lives. They sang for the birth of their children and at the death of their loved ones. They sang when they planted or when they hunted well.

Today, songs are still tremendously important to all peoples. Every one of the thousands of different societies on Earth has its own songs. In this, we are all the same.

The songs in this book come from different tribal peoples all over the world: the native peoples of the Americas, the Aborigines of Australia, and many of the peoples who live in Asia and Africa.

What is a tribe? It is like a collection of huge families, with lots of cousins, aunts, grandparents, even great-grandparents. They speak the same language, know the same ceremonies, and look after one another. Some tribes are very large, a million or more people; some are tiny and number only a hundred or so. Most tribal peoples have lived in the same places for so long that they are closely associated with them and are considered native, or indigenous, peoples. But tribes do not actually call themselves tribal peoples. Their own name is usually a word that simply means "people" in their own language.

Tribal peoples often have their own economic systems. Some of them live without using money. They get their food from their animals, from growing crops, from gathering wild fruits and berries, or from hunting or fishing. They build their homes out of the natural materials that are

nearby: wood, leaves, animal hides, and dried mud. Some have no houses at all; they live in shelters erected in just a few minutes. They have their own medicines, made from plants, and their own ways of teaching their children.

Some people think that tribes live as our ancient ancestors did. But they are not old-fashioned, backward, or ignorant. In fact, they live in today's world just as we do, and they use their skills creatively to adapt and change things, just as we do. Tribal life may appear simple but it is not really. Tribes have found expert ways to live in some of the most difficult places on Earth, from the hottest deserts to the freezing Arctic.

Tribal peoples who live off the land around them don't work in the kind of jobs many of us do, leaving their homes to go to an office or factory. Because their work is close to home and because they can often do it skillfully and quickly, they have more time each day to tell stories, play with and teach their children, discuss news, and celebrate their religious beliefs. And singing is often a part of these activities.

Some people think that tribal life is better—even more advanced—than our own. After all, as well as having to spend less time working than we do, tribal people are not as likely to be lonely since they live in close-knit groups where everyone, old and young, is cared for. And most tribes have developed extraordinarily efficient ways of life that make intelligent use of our Earth.

Tribal people rely on each other and the land to survive. They can help to remind us that we must respect those who are different from ourselves and constantly strive to live in harmony with the Earth and all people everywhere. The songs in this collection help us to see how different tribes honor and celebrate the world we all share.

Stephen Corry *Survival International*

BEGINNINGS

Long before words were written, communities sang of their lives and how they began. They sang of the making of the Earth, the coming of the sun, the birth of a baby, and the growing of new plants.

Many of these songs are still sung today by tribal peoples. The Pima of North America sing of the Earth Magician making the mountains. For the Fang people of Africa, the sun arrives each day with a quiver full of lighted arrows. In the desert of the Tewa Indians, the rain hangs in the air like a weaving loom. The clothing that is woven by the loom is the green of the land after the new rainfall.

Reading the songs in this section, we can celebrate the beginnings that are important to people everywhere. The Nootka, from North America, sing, "You, whose day it is, make it beautiful." So, this new day is your day; it is your choice — make it beautiful.

THE SPIRIT OF SONG

Aztec, Central America

In the true spirit of song
I lift my voice through a trumpet of gold,
I let fall from my lips a celestial song.

I shall speak notes precious and brilliant
as those of the miaua bird,
I shall bring to blossom a new song.

I lift my voice like the burning incense of flowers,
so that I the singer
may cause joy before the
    face of the Cause of All.

As he starts his song, this Aztec celebrates the power and beauty of language by comparing his voice to a bird song and to the blossoming of flowers.

SONG OF THE LOOM

Tewa, North America

O our Mother the earth, O our Father the sky,
Your children are we, and with tired backs
We bring you the gifts you love.

Then weave for us a garment
of brightness:

May the warp be the white light
of morning,
May the weft be the red light
of evening,
May the fringes be the falling rain,
May the border be the standing
rainbow.

Thus weave for us a garment
of brightness,
That we may walk fittingly where birds sing,
That we may walk fittingly where grass is green.

O our Mother the earth, O our Father the sky.

10

SONG TO THE SUN

Fang, Africa

The fearful night sinks
Trembling into the depth
Before your lightning eye
And the rapid arrows
From your fiery quiver.
With sparking blows of light
You tear her cloak
The black cloak lined with fire
And studded with gleaming stars —
With sparking blows of light
You tear the black cloak.

In this song, the sun is addressed as though it were a hunter, whose arrows pierce the cloak of the night sky — who is regarded as a woman — so that the new day can begin.

THE CREATION OF EARTH

Pima, North America

Earth Magician shapes this world,
    Behold what he can do!
Round and smooth he molds it,
    Behold what he can do!
Earth Magician makes the mountains,
    Heed what he has to say!
He it is that makes the mesas,
    Heed what he has to say!
Earth Magician shapes this world;
Earth Magician makes its mountains;
Makes all larger, larger, larger.
    Into the earth the Magician glances;
Into its mountains he may see.

A mesa *is a flat-topped mountain or hill.*

VOICES THAT BEAUTIFY THE EARTH

Cherokee, North America

Voice above,
Voice of Thunder,
Speak from the dark of clouds;
Voice below,
Grasshopper-voice,
Speak from the green of plants;
So may the earth be beautiful.

THE CYCLE OF A'ASIA

Papua New Guinea, Australasia

Water all over
all all over

Darkness all over
all all over

Aia sitting seated
Aia living alive

Aia sitting seated
sitting forever
Aia living alive
living forever

Aia without beginning
Aia without end

Above the water
Aia has lived
Aia has watched

Aia has watched
above the darkness

Aia has lived
Aia has watched

Aia creator of our earth
Aia creator of our home

*In this song, Aia is the creator of the earth
and is without beginning or end.*

AWAY IN THE EAST

Zuni, North America

Away in the east,
the rain clouds care for the little corn plants
as a mother cares for her baby.

SONG OF THE FLOOD

Navajo, North America

The first man — you are his child, he is your child.

The first woman — you are his child, he is your child.

The water monster — you are his child, he is your child.

The black sea-horse — you are his child, he is your child.

The black snake — you are his child, he is your child.

The big blue snake — you are his child, he is your child.

The white corn — you are his child, he is your child.

The yellow corn — you are his child, he is your child.

The corn pollen — you are his child, he is your child.

The corn beetle — you are his child, he is your child.

Sahanahray — you are his child, he is your child.

Bekayhozhon — you are his child, he is your child.

The connection between all living things — human beings, animals, and plants — from the beginning of time to the present day, is given special emphasis in the repeated choruses of this Navajo song.

WHO HAS MADE THE EARTH?

Santal, Asia

Who has made the earth?
Oh, who has made the cows?
Thakur made the earth.
Thakur made the cows.

During the Sohrae festival, which takes place in December or January and which celebrates cattle and fertility, a band of three drummers with one or two singers go from cow shed to cow shed late in the evening and sing this song to the cows. Thakur means "the Creator."

▶ ✖ ◆ ✖ ◆ ✖ ◆ ✖ ◀

CHINOOK BLESSING

Chinook, North America

We call upon the earth, our planet home, with its beautiful depths and soaring heights, its vitality and abundance of life, and together we ask that it

teach us, and show us the Way

We call upon the creatures of the fields and forests and seas, our brothers and sisters the wolves and deer, the eagle and dove, the great whales and the dolphins, the beautiful orca and salmon who share our Northwest home, and we ask them to

teach us, and show us the Way

We call upon all those who have lived on this earth, our ancestors and our friends, who dreamed the best for future generations, and upon whose lives our lives are built, and with thanksgiving we call upon them to

teach us, and show us the Way

An orca *is a kind of whale.*

WHEN THE CHILD IS NAMED

Tewa, North America

The mother and the grandmother stand on the housetop before dawn; the grandmother speaks:

My sun!
My morning star!
Help this child to become a man.
I name him
Rain-dew Falling!
I name him
Star Mountain!

The mother throws a live coal; the grandmother throws a sacred meal.

In this song, when the baby is named, a live coal and a corn cob are thrown. They signify life and health. The song is offered to the sun and the morning star.

SONG TO BRING FAIR WEATHER

Nootka, North America

You, whose day it is, make it beautiful.
Get out your rainbow colors,
So it will be beautiful.

THE LIVING WORLD

In tribal communities, the lives of animals and people are closely connected. Animals are important as a source of food, labor, and materials, and because their living patterns help humans to keep track of the days and the seasons; but they also have a spiritual significance.

The Arrente of Australasia sing of their holy ancestors as ant workers. The Shuar weaver, from South America, describes himself as a spider spinning textiles that are strong and durable.

For herding communities — who depend on animals and not on crops for their food — cows, sheep, and goats are a sign of wealth and status. You can see how important the bull is for the Dinka poet who says his bull "shines like the morning star."

In these songs you will read of animals but also of people and their lives — their working days, special occasions, games, and dreams. People everywhere give thanks for the living world. Reading these songs helps us to realize that what is important to us is also important to all peoples.

THE OWL

Hopi, North America

The owl hooted
and told of the morning star.
He hooted again
and told of the dawn.

23

I RISE FROM MY BED

Inuit, North America

I rise from my bed
with arms outspread
like the wings of the swift raven

I rise
to greet the day
way! way!

I turn my face from the black night
and watch the dawn come white

casting off in my canoe
I think of trifles
of my daily life

how great they seem
how great the torment
of each day's demands

yet only one thing
is great;
to see from my home

the day coming
the day being born
the light filling the world

SEAGULL

Netsilik, North America

SEAGULL
who flaps his wings
over my head
        in the blue air

you GULL up there
dive down
        come here
take me with you
        in the air!

Wings flash by
in my mind's eye
and I'm up there sailing
in the cool air
        a-a-a-a-a-ah
          in the air.

A WOLF, MAYBE TWO WOLVES

Seneca, North America

Yo
w
e
e
e
e
e
e
e
e
e
e
e
e
e

He comes running
across the field where
he comes running

e
e
e
e
e
e
Y
e
e
o
w
e
e
e
e
e
e
e
e
e
e
e
e

he comes running
across the field where
he comes running

27

SPARROWHAWK

Quechua, South America

Sparrowhawk of the sky, falcon of the heights
come down a little while
I am lost in these mountains
carry me on your wings to the road

I am lost in these mountains
sparrowhawk of the heights
I only want you to carry me to the road
come down a little while, sky falcon

Leave me on the road, falcon
from there I could go on with the travelers
with the crowd of villagers
sparrowhawk, come down a little while

CHOOSE THEM

Ewe, Africa

Choose them, do not discriminate,
Choose them.
Even the uncomely ones,
Choose them.
Even the flat-bottomed ones,
Choose them.
Even wearers of insufficient beads,
Choose them.
Even the dirty, thin-legged ones,
Choose them.
Do not discriminate,
Choose them.

THRESHING SONG

Quechua, South America

Let us go around, let us go around
Clap hands
Let us follow the crowd, let us follow the crowd
Clap hands
Beside the threshing floor
Clap hands
Beside this threshing floor we will have a circle
Clap hands
Let us have rods of ribbons
Clap hands
Let us increase, let us stretch out with the shawl
Clap hands
We will spread out the matting, let us spread out
Clap hands
Like rain let us shower down, let us shower down
Clap hands
Like rain let us spread out, let us spread out
Clap hands

To clap, to run, is to learn how
Clap hands
Strike at it, strike at it
Clap hands
Dance more, dance more
Clap hands
Beside this threshing floor
Clap hands

During the harvest, it is the custom for the Quechua peoples to have a threshing party. Young men and women are chosen by the farmer. They play a game of chase, running across the corn or wheat while others sing and clap this song. When the game is over, the grains can be separated from their husks.

THE ANT WORKERS

Arrente, Australasia

The ant workers yonder dwell, ever dwell;
In ring-tiered homes, they dwell, ever dwell.

With down-hooded heads they dwell, ever dwell;
With stripe-banded chests they dwell, ever dwell.

With cobweb-closed eyes they dwell, ever dwell;
With down-hooded heads they dwell, ever dwell.

In cellared cells they dwell, ever dwell;
With bodies ring-rimm'd they dwell, ever dwell.

In cellared cells they dwell, ever dwell;
Like pebbles pile-heap'd they dwell, ever dwell.

Where far-flung their hollows stretch
With firelight aglow they dwell, ever dwell.

Where far-flung their hollows stretch
With firelight aflame they dwell, ever dwell.

CROCODILE! CROCODILE!

Khon Thai, Asia

Crocodile! Crocodile!
Swimming by the teak mill,
Your teeth are all broken;
You can't bite us!

This song is sung by children in central Thailand when they are playing a riverside game of tag. One player is the crocodile, who stays on the low ground (a river). Other players stay on higher ground (the river bank) but dart in and out of the "river," The crocodile tries to tag them. Anyone who is tagged is "dead" and has to be the crocodile. While in the "river," the players tease the crocodile by chanting this song.

I'LL RETURN AGAIN

Garifuna, Central America

Before I went aboard the boat,
I had a talk with my younger brother.
Before my chat was over,
I was shedding tears.
Brother, have no fears for me.
I'll return again,
You'll see me again.

Chorus
I'll not abandon my homeland.
My footprints are there by my parents' door.
My relatives are there,
I'll visit from time to time.
I'll come home to seek my town.

ELEPHANT

Yoruba, Africa

Elephant, who brings death.
Elephant, a spirit in the bush,
The spirit who eats
A whole palm fruit with its thorns.
With a single hand
He can pull two palm trees to the ground.
If he had two hands
He would tear the sky like an old rag.
   With his four mortal legs
     He tramples down the grass.
    Wherever he walks
    The grass is forbidden to
      stand up again.

COCONUT SONG

Swahili, Africa

Dry fronds of the coconut palm.
When they catch the
wind it blows them.
Blows! Blows! Blows!

*Children sing this song
while playing a game in
which they move counter-
clockwise in a circle with
their arms in the air,
waving like the fronds of the
coconut palm. When they
sing "Blows! Blows! Blows!"
they wave their arms even more and,
on the last "Blows!", fall to the ground.*

SPINNING SONG

Shuar, South America

For me it is very easy
To spin yarn.
For I am a man-spider.
I am a man-spider.
Therefore I am adept.

My hand is like the hand
Of a spider.
Because of this,
I make the spindle hum.

*In Shuar society, men do the spinning,
dyeing, and weaving. The yarn is spun
from homegrown cotton and dyed in
vegetable solutions. A special type of clay
is sometimes rubbed into the wet yarn to
produce dark shades.*

ZEBRA

Shona, Africa

Thank you, Zebra,
Adorned with your own stripes,
Iridescent and glittering creature,
Whose skin is as soft as a girl's is;
One on which the eye dwells all day, as on the solitary cow of a poor man;
Creature that makes the forests beautiful,
Weaver of lines,
Who wear your skin for display,
Drawn with lines so clearly defined;
You who thread beads in patterns,
Dappled fish,
Hatching round the neck of a pot;
Beauty spots cut to rise in a crescent on the forehead,
A patterned belt for the waist;
Light reflected,
Dazzling the eyes.

It is its own instinct, the Zebra's,

Adorned as if with strings of beads around the waist as women are;

Wild creature without anger or any grudge,

Lineage with a totem that is nowhere a stranger,

Line that stretches everywhere,

Owners of the land.

Zebras were traditionally hunted for food, and this song shows the respect for the hunter's opponent.
They are also held in awe and celebrated in sacred rites.

THE MAGNIFICENT BULL

Dinka, Africa

My bull is white like the silver fish in the river
White like the shimmering crane bird on the river bank
White like fresh milk!
His roar is like the thunder of the Turkish cannon on the steep shore.
My bull is dark like the rain cloud in the storm.
He is like summer and winter
Half of him is dark like the storm cloud,
Half of him is light like sunshine.
His back shines like the morning star.
His brow is red like the beak of the hornbill.
His forehead is like a flag, calling the people from a distance,
He resembles the rainbow.

I will water him at the river,
With my spear I shall drive away my enemies.
Let them water their herds at the well;
The river belongs to me and my bull.
Drink, my bull, from the river; I am here
To guard you with my spear.

Parts of Africa were under the rule of the Turkish during the time of the Ottoman Empire.

RIDDLES

Santal, Asia

The big house with the single pole — A bamboo umbrella

Two men who are always beating each other — The lips

The boy who cries when he is kissed — A flute

Two men who sit on one stool but do not touch each other —
    Pots on a hearth

A sickle hangs in the sky — The new moon

The dark girl who never has a bath —
    A pot for frying maize

YOU ARE MINE

Asante, Africa

Someone would like to have you for her child
but you are mine.
Someone would like to rear you on a costly mat
but you are mine.
Someone would like to place you on a camel blanket
but you are mine.
I have you to rear on a torn old mat.
Someone would like to have you as her child
but you are mine.

LULLABY

Baka "Pygmy," Africa

Sleep, sleep, little one;
Close your eyes, sleep, little one!
The night comes down, the hour has come,
Tomorrow it will be day.
Sleep, sleep, little one!
On your closed eyes day has fled.

You are warm. You have drunk,
Sleep, sleep, little one!
Sleep, tomorrow you will be big, you will be strong.
Sleep, tomorrow you will take the bow and the knife.

Sleep, you will be strong,
You will be straight, and I bent.
Sleep, tomorrow it is you,
but it is mother always.

THE ELEMENTS

Water, fire, earth, and air were long believed to be the four elements of which the world was made. We are reminded of how essential they are to our lives when we remember that without rain we cannot drink, without the sun we cannot be warm, without earth we cannot grow food, and without air we cannot breathe.

In these songs, the elements are associated with the Creator of the Earth. For the Khoekhoe from Africa, the rainbow is the Creator's hunting bow, which sparkles as he sets out to collect the stars in his basket until it overflows with light and morning arrives. The Quechua from South America sing to the Great Sun to "wake the seeds and make them grow," while the Bhil of Asia call to the rain god to bring rain so the crops may be plentiful.

Natural things around us can remind us of our place in the world and of our own strengths. If we feel small, we can remember the wind in the Hausa poem: Even though the wind has no weight, it can cut down the biggest tree.

THE ROCK

Cherokee, North America

The rock lies near
While light comes and goes
Said to have no soul
The rock cannot be sad
It knows not the time
It has no life to hold
It can't feel love
As we admire it
It remains in stillness
Yet in its own way
May watch

SACRED SEED SONG

Quechua, South America

Men:
Ayau Hailli, ayau Hailli!
Great Sun, mighty Father,
Wake the seeds and make them grow.

Women:
Hailli, Pachamama, Hailli
Hailli, O Earth Mother, Hailli

For the Quechua peoples, the land is tilled at the command of the sun, with the cooperation of Mother Earth. At sowing time, the men break up the earth with foot ploughs and the women plant the seed in time to this sacred song.

THERE IS JOY

Inuit, North America

There is joy in
Feeling the warmth
Come to the great world
And seeing the sun
Follow its old footprints
In the summer night

There is fear in
Feeling the cold
Come to the great world
And seeing the moon
Now new moon, now full moon
Follow its old footprints
In the winter night

The Inuit survive in one of the harshest climates in the world. This song expresses their feelings at the coming of summer, which is very short, and at the onset of winter, when for many dark months, they will see only the moon.

WIND

Hausa, Africa

O wind, you have no weight,
but you cut down the biggest trees.

SONG FOR THE SUN THAT DISAPPEARED BEHIND THE RAIN CLOUDS

Khoekhoe, Africa

The fire darkens, the wood turns black.

The flame extinguishes, misfortune is upon us.

God sets out in search of the sun.

The rainbow sparkles in his hand,

The bow of the divine hunter.

He has heard the lamentations of his children.

He walks along the Milky Way, he collects the stars.

With quick arms he piles them into a basket,

Piles them up with quick arms

Like a woman who collects lizards

And piles them into her pot, piles them

Until the pot overflows
   with lizards

Until the basket overflows
   with light.

RAINDROP

Tswana, Africa

Little
rainy raindrop
when
will
you
drop
drop
drop?

THE RAIN GOD

Bhil, Asia

O rain god,
Please, bring to my land
Prosperity, rich crops,
corn and cucumber.

RAINBOW

"Pygmy," Africa

Rainbow rainbow
shining high so high
above the great forest
and black clouds
dividing the dark sky

O conqueror
you have poured down
the growling thunder
loud with rage
was he angry with us?

amid the black clouds
dividing the dark sky
as the knife cuts the ripe fruit
rainbow rainbow

the thunder the man-killer
fled like the antelope
before the panther
he fled
rainbow rainbow

strongbow
of the Great Hunter
who hunts the clouds like a herd
of frightened elephants
rainbow give him our thanks

say DO NOT BE ANGRY
say DO NOT KILL US
for we are full of fear
rainbow tell him

STAR SONG

Baka "Pygmy," Africa

Glittering stars of the white night,
Moon shining on high,
Piercing the forest with your pale beams,
Stars, friends of white ghosts,
Moon, their protectress!

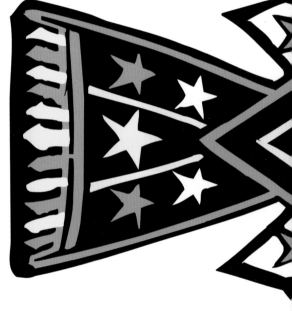

BIRDS OF FIRE

Passamaquoddy, North America

We are the stars which sing.
We sing with our light.
We are the birds of fire.
We fly across the heaven.

THE NIGHT

Fipa, Africa

The night is over
before one has finished counting the stars.

*Fipa proverbs like this one are told to children to help them understand the
world around them. This one means that the universe is far too great to be
understood by any one person.*

SURVIVAL

Tribal communities survive in some of the harshest climates of the world. They have endured floods and famines, droughts and earthquakes. And they have songs to give them the strength and courage to face such natural dangers. But now there is a greater threat to their livelihood — losing their land.

Take land from tribal people and you take their food, medicine, building materials, and the everyday things that give their lives spiritual significance. Land is lost when new roads or factories are built, where river valleys are flooded or forests are cut down. The Xingu poet from South America whose land is gone sings, "My rainbow rises over sand; my river falls on stone."

We can forget how the land, its creatures, plants, and elements help all of us to live; if we are careless about our environment, then we will not survive. The Yoruba poet from Africa cautions us to "enjoy the earth gently," and the Omaha poet from North America reminds us that we shall vanish one day, but the land will remain.

PROPHECY

Maya, Central America

Eat, eat, thou hast bread;
Drink, drink, thou hast water;
On that day, dust possesses the earth,
On that day, a cloud rises,

On that day, a mountain rises,
On that day, a strong man seizes the land,
On that day, things fall to ruin,
On that day, the tender leaf is destroyed,
On that day, the dying eyes are closed,
On that day, three signs are on the tree,
On that day, three generations hang there,
On that day, the battle flag is raised,
And they are scatter'd afar in the forests.

This writer is warning of a time when the natural order of the Earth might be destroyed.

I SHALL VANISH

Omaha, North America

I shall vanish and be no more,
But the land over which I now roam
Shall remain
And change not.

ENJOY THE EARTH

Yoruba, Africa

Enjoy the earth gently
Enjoy the earth gently
For if the earth is spoiled
It cannot be repaired
Enjoy the earth gently

THE GREAT FAMINE

Bhil, Asia

The great neem trees have withered away
The river beds are dry as dust
The children of the Bhil are starving
A great and severe famine has come
And spread all over the land
Then the monsoon clouds appear
And signs of rain can be seen
The rivers begin to flow again
The neem trees turn
    green once again
The trees in the
jungle too are green
The barns are full
    of grain

*In order to survive, the Bhil must rely on the monsoon rains
coming in time to bring water for them and their crops.*

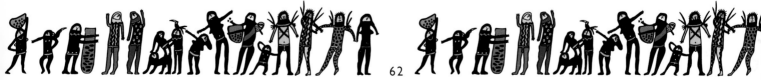

RICE FIELDS

Adivasi, Asia

Our rice fields, the *tilae*,
are under fire, my beloved
Oh, where shall we eat now, manaju my beloved,
where shall we feed?

*Some of the tribal people of India have watched as
their beautiful terraced rice fields — named after the
tilae, a flower — have slipped into the hands of others.
Their wish is to live from the land, to love it, and be
trusted to care for it.* Manaju *means "beloved."*

THEY HAVE STOLEN MY LAND

Xingu, South America

They have stolen my land;
the birds have flown,
my people gone.
My rainbow rises over sand;
my river falls on stone.

MAGIC SONG

To be recited when in sudden danger

Inuit, North America

You earth,
Our great earth!
See, oh see:
All these heaps
Of bleached bones
And wind-dried skeletons!
They crumble in the air,
The mighty world,
The mighty world's
Air!
Bleached bones,
Wind-dried skeletons,
Crumble in the air!
Hey-hey-hey!

NO ONE CAN GET NEAR MY HOUSE

Shuar, South America

I am like a snake.
No one can get near my house,
Because there is a lake around it.
I am a jaguar,
The bravest that is,
And no one
Can get near my house.

*This is sung by a man to his enemies when he believes
that they are about to attack.*

THIS LAND

Akawaio, South America

This land is where we belong
This land is where we are at home, we know its ways
This land is needed for those who come after
We know where to find all this land provides for us
This land keeps us together within its mountains

SONG FOR A WHALE

Aborigine, Australasia

What is that which blocks us? The whale!
As we paddle, we see its gaping mouth. What is that?
Spray and sea splash as it moves;
We paddle gently, for we see the open mouth of the whale.
Water rises and swirls, with noise caused by the whale:
spray and foam from the whale
As we paddle, we see it swimming.
Bralbral calls to the Djanggawul;
Let us take some.
The others we leave in the sea.

In some areas of the world, communities depend on the sea for their food supply. Hunters are careful never to take more than they need. It is only since whaling has been carried out by huge ships that whales have been threatened with extinction. Pollution is also a major threat to the survival of whales and other sea creatures.

MAY A GOOD WIND BE YOUR ROAD

Omaha, North America

Naked you came from Earth the Mother.
Naked you return to her.
May a good wind be your road.

WHAT IS HAPPINESS?

Santal, Asia

In life, what is happiness?
In life, what is joy?
To be in love with others,
For when we die,
We go with no one.

OUR CHILDREN'S EARTH

Nomadic Pastoralists, Africa

Treat the earth well.
It was not given to us by our fathers,
But is lent to us by our children.

MAORI CHANT

Maori, Australasia

We need our *marae* for many reasons:
That we may rise tall in oratory.
That we may weep for our dead.
That we may pray to God.
That we may have our feasts.
That we may house our guests.
That we may have our meetings.
That we may have our weddings.
That we may have our reunions.
That we may sing.
That we may dance.
And there find the richness of life
And the proud heritage that is truly ours.

The marae *is the traditional Maori meeting place.*

MY FLOWERS

Aztec, Central America

My flowers will not come to an end,
my songs will not come to an end.
I, the singer, raise them up;
they are scattered, they are bestowed.
Even though flowers on earth
may wither and yellow,
they will be carried there
to the interior of the house
of the bird with the golden
    feathers.

*The Aztec poet believes that the person who understands
flowers and songs can begin to understand the mysteries surrounding
the Giver of Life.*

ABOUT THE TRIBES

NORTH AMERICA

Most tribal peoples in North, Central, and South America are usually called "Indians," but many in the United States prefer to be known as "Native Americans." The Inuit of the far north are often called "Eskimo," but they do not like the name. They include the Netsilik of the central Arctic.

These native peoples once lived throughout what is now Canada and the United States — from the icy north, through the woodlands and grass plains, all the way south to the burning deserts near Mexico. The Omaha hunted the bison that roamed the prairies. The Cherokee, Seneca, and Passamaquoddy were farmers. The Chinook were fisher folk, as were coastal peoples, like the Nootka, who carved impressive totem poles. The Hopi, Zuni, Tewa, Pima, and Navajo thrived in the desert, growing corn and beans, and hunting for food.

Many native peoples still hunt, fish, or farm today, but others live in cities — often in poor areas. Their land was taken from them, and they have become the poorest people in two of the world's richest countries.

CENTRAL AMERICA

Most people in Central America are descended from Indians, though many have been made to feel ashamed of this. The Aztec and Maya empires flourished there until the Spanish conquerors destroyed them. The surviving Indians are mostly poor hill farmers who have seen their best land stolen by settlers. Others, like the Garifuna, live in the tropical rain forests. Civil wars recently killed thousands of Indians in Central America.

SOUTH AMERICA

Many South American Indians live in Amazonia, the largest rain forest on Earth. These include the different Xingu tribes in Brazil, the Akawaio of Guyana, and the Shuar of Ecuador. Many others live in the vast grass plains in the north, or the scrub lands in the south of the continent. In addition, millions of Indians, mostly Quechua and Aymara, live in the Andes mountains. Until the Europeans came and conquered them five hundred years ago, their ancestors formed the Inca empire.

The mountain Indians are very poor; most of their best land has now been taken. In the Amazon, the Indians are today being invaded by ranchers and mining companies. Their forest home is being destroyed, and many are dying from illnesses brought in by the newcomers.

AFRICA

The word *tribe* is often considered insulting in Africa because people think it means "backward." But there are many peoples living where their ancestors made their homes centuries ago. Now they often call themselves "indigenous" peoples, which means "belonging to a place."

There are many indigenous peoples scattered throughout the continent, including the tribes usually called "Pygmies" (because they tend to be shorter than other peoples), who live mostly in the forests of central and west Africa, and the Bushman tribes who live in and around the Kalahari Desert.

Many of the larger tribes are nomadic pastoralists, like the famous Maasai of east Africa, living with their herds of cattle and goats.

The peoples mentioned in this book are: the Dinka from Sudan; Fang, "Pygmy," Asante, Ewe, Yoruba, and Hausa from west Africa; Swahili and Fipa from east Africa; and Shona, Tswana, and Khoekhoe from southern Africa.

Many indigenous peoples have seen their land taken from them, and in some countries they have been attacked and killed.

ASIA

Many tribes live in the hot tropical forests of southeast Asia, where they hunt and grow crops. At the other extreme, in Siberian Russia, the ground is frozen for most of the year and practically nothing grows. There the tribes live by reindeer-herding and fishing.

There are also many tribes in India. They are called Adivasis and were there before the present-day Indians arrived. One of the most important Adivasi tribes is the Santal — rice-growing hill farmers who are famous for their dances and music. Most Adivasis face problems similar to tribal peoples everywhere: their land is being taken from them. The Bhil in western India are suffering as their homes and fields are flooded as the result of the construction of a huge dam.

AUSTRALASIA

Australasia is a geographic term that denotes New Zealand and many other islands of the southwest Pacific, as well as Australia itself. Tribal peoples once lived in most of these islands and in many cases they still do. They vary from the rain forest–dwelling peoples of New Guinea to the different Aborigine tribes of Australia who once dwelled on the coast and in the forests as well as in the huge desert interior. They have been there longer than any other people are known to have lived anywhere else. Their ancestors were there at least 40,000 years ago. (That's 35,000 years before the Egyptian pyramids and Stonehenge were built!) The Arrente are just one of the hundreds of different Aboriginal peoples. In New Zealand there are still many of one tribal people — the Maori — who were there before the British settlers arrived.

In some countries, such as Indonesia, tribal peoples are killed for trying to keep their land. In Australia, many Aboriginal peoples are now very poor and live close to towns. Like the native peoples of North America, they too are the poorest people in a rich country.

INFORMATION ON
SURVIVAL INTERNATIONAL

If you want to help ensure that tribal peoples survive, you can do so through Survival International. Supporters of this organization believe that the lives and lands of tribal peoples should be respected.

Did you know that many of our medicines originally came from plants, and that they were first discovered by tribal peoples? Tribal peoples often know far more about plant life than we do. Indeed, many of the vegetables that we eat today were first discovered by tribes who found out how to crossbreed different plants to produce new or better types.

Can you imagine a world without french fries and ketchup? If it hadn't been for the Indians in the Andes mountains, we wouldn't have potatoes. They not only discovered how to grow large, healthy potatoes, they also found a way to freeze-dry them so that they would keep for months without going rotten. This enabled the Indians to eat well during the lean months between harvests. They still do this today. In addition, Central American tribes were the first to grow tomatoes. When Europeans first saw them, they thought they were a kind of apple and called them "love apples."

Without the Amazon Indians we might not have basketballs either! They discovered how to make rubber from the sap of a special kind of tree and were playing with rubbers balls centuries before anyone else.

In spite of all the things that tribal peoples have given us, they are not being allowed to live as they choose. They are being forced from their homes and killed because other people want their land. Some of the worst offenders are mining and logging companies. Another big problem is that governments encourage ranchers and city dwellers to move on to tribal land, set up new towns, and take over completely. In addition, the settlers sometimes introduce new diseases to the tribes that can be fatal to them. Colds and the flu, for example, may be only mild illnesses to us, but they can wipe out whole tribes.

Survival International is an organization of people who want to stop these crimes from taking place, and who believe that tribes should be able to live on their own land — in peace. It believes that they should be given the same chance as the rest of us to adapt and change as they think best.

Survival International engages in many activities to support tribal peoples. It pays for the medicines urgently needed for health and vaccination programs, as well as funding the tribes' own projects and organizations. Some members of Survival write letters to those responsible for stealing the land of tribal peoples and for ignoring their rights. Survival also helps representatives from the tribes to put their case to the rest of the world. Tribal peoples know best what they need in order to survive, and instead of explaining things for them. Survival helps them to speak for themselves. Survival International has proved, time and time again, that ordinary people can make a big difference in the way tribal peoples are treated.

If you want to help tribal peoples yourself, you can write to Survival International at the address below and ask them for more information about what you can do.

Stephen Corry, *Director*, **Survival International**, (Dept. BB), 11–15 Emerald Street, London WC1N 3QL, United Kingdom. Telephone: 171–242 1441 Fax: 171–242 1771

INDEX OF FIRST LINES

ARTIST'S ACKNOWLEDGMENTS

The great range of tribal art is as rich as the verbal tradition from which these songs have been selected. The museums and libraries of the world have yet to cover much of this vast storehouse of images. My main challenge in the absence of specific source material was to create an overall style to illustrate such a varied collection of subjects and cultures. Because so much tribal art is craft-based, I decided to cut my designs in linoleum. In recent years, especially in the South African townships, this humble flooring material has been the basis of some vigorous printmaking. For me in particular, the lino-cuts of the Namibian artist John Muafangejo have been a great inspiration.

Bernard Lodge

COMPILER'S ACKNOWLEDGMENTS

Finding the songs for this book was an exciting but not an easy task for me, as many tribal peoples have not written their songs down. I am, of course, very glad that some have been recorded, so that we can read them now. I would like to thank all those who have helped me with this project, in particular Wilson Primary School, Reading, where I began my search; The School of Oriental and African Studies, London; The Bhavan Institute of Indian Art and Culture, London; and the Hispanic and Luso Brazilian Council Library, London. I would also like to thank Jeff Kenna, our son Jamie, and all the friends who have supported this work.

Nikki Siegen-Smith

PUBLISHER'S ACKNOWLEDGMENTS

Grateful acknowledgement is made to the following for permission to print the material listed below.

Abecadarius Books: for *"Raindrop,"* an excerpt from *Sechuana Proverbs* by the first black South African novelist, Sol Plaatje (1875–1932). Copyright © 1988 by Abecadarius Books. **American Anthropological Association, Arlington, U.S.A.:** for *"The Creation of Earth,"* originally titled "The Creation of the Earth," reprinted from *The Pima Indians* by Frank Russell, American Ethnology Bulletin 1904–5. Not for further reproduction. **Arthur Barker** and **Weidenfeld and Nicolson:** for *"Magic Song,"* from *The Book of Eskimos*. **Columbia University Press:** for *"May a Good Wind Be Your Road,"* originally titled "Prayer to the Deceased," from *Omaha Secret Societies* by R. F. Fortune. Copyright © 1932 by Columbia University Press. **Ghana Publishing Corporation:** for *"Choose Them,"* reproduced from E. Y. Egblowogbe's *Games and Songs as Education Media*, published in 1975 by the Ghana Publishing Corporation. **Kegan Paul International:** for *"Wind,"* an excerpt from *Hausa Proverbs* by Captain G. Merrick, published in 1905 by Kegan Paul, Trench, Trubner & Co. Ltd. **Mahipal Publications:** for *"The Rain God"* and *"The Great Famine,"* from *The Book of Bhil Poetry from Ghillare*, 1979. Copyright by, and reprinted by permission of, Mahipal Bhuriya. **University of Nebraska Press:** for *"Song of the Flood,"* *"The Owl,"* and *"The Spirit of Song,"* originally titled "An Otomi Song of the Mexicans," reprinted from *The Sky Clears*, by A. Grove Day, by permission of the University of Nebraska Press. Copyright ©1951 by A. Grove Day. **University of Oklahoma Press:** for *"My Flowers,"* an excerpt from *Fifteen Poets of the Aztec World* by Miguel Leon-Portilla. Copyright © 1992 by the University of Oklahoma Press. **Oxford University Press:** for *"Away in the East"* and *"Enjoy the Earth,"* originally titled "Nicely, nicely" and "Yoruba Poem" from *Earthways Earthwise — Poems on Conservation*, selected by Judith Nicholls, OUP, 1993; for *"The Night,"* an excerpt from *Gold and Gods of Peru*, by Hans Baumann, OUP and Random House Inc.,1963; for *Zebra*, an excerpt from *Shona Praise Poetry*, compiled by A. C. Hodza, edited and translated by G. P. Fortune, OUP 1979. **Sunstone Press:** for *"When the Child Is Named."* This poem from *Songs of the Tewa,* collected and translated by Herbert Joseph Spinden, appears courtesy of *Sunstone Press*, Box 2321, Santa Fe, NM 87504-2321, U.S.A.

Other material included in this collection has been taken from the following sources:

Alfred van der Marck Editions: *"A Wolf, Maybe Two Wolves,"* originally titled "A Poem About a Wolf, Maybe Two Wolves," from *Shaking the Pumpkin*, edited by Jerome Rothenberg, 1986. **Collins, Angus & Robertson:** *"I Rise from My Bed"* and *"Rainbow,"* excerpts translated by Keith Bosley and reprinted from *And I Dance*, 1972. **Cambridge University Press:** *"Song to the Sun,"* originally titled "Hymn to the Sun," *"You Are Mine,"* originally titled "Lullaby," *"The Magnificent Bull,"* *"Song for the Sun That Disappeared Behind the Rainclouds,"* reprinted from *African Poetry*, edited by Ulli Beier, 1970. **Education Development Center, Inc., Cambridge, Massachusetts:** *"Seagull,"* originally titled "Magic Words to Feel Better," reprinted from *Songs and Stories of the Netsilik Eskimos* by Edward Field, published in 1967, 1968. **Faber and Faber Limited:** *"Prophecy,"* *"They Have Stolen My Land,"* originally titled "Song of the Xingu Indian," reprinted from *What on Earth…?*, edited by Judith Nicholls, 1989. **George Allen & Unwin Ltd:** *"Who Has Made the Earth?"* *"Riddles,"* *"What Is Happiness?"* excerpts reprinted from *The Hill of Flutes, Life, Love and Poetry in Tribal India*, by W. G. Archer, 1974. **Grosset & Dunlap, Inc.:** *"There Is Joy,"* from *Out of the Earth I Sing*, edited by Richard Lewis, 1968. **Rider Books:** *"Chinook Blessing,"* originally titled "Chinook Blessing Litany" and *"Maori Chant,"* originally titled "Maori Greeting Chant," reprinted from *The Way*, by Edward Goldsmith, 1990. **Robert Hale & Company:** *"Spinning Song,"* *"No One Can Get Near My House,"* excerpts reprinted from *The Jivaro* by Michael J. Harner, 1973. **Routledge & Kegan Paul Ltd:** *"Song for a Whale,"* excerpt reprinted from *Djanggawul, An Aboriginal Religious Cult of North-Eastern Arnham Land*, by Ronald M. Berndt, 1952. **Sanders and Peek:** *"Song to Bring Fair Weather,"* reprinted from *Literature of the American Indian*. **Sun Books:** *"The Cycle of A'aisa,"* reprinted from *Words of Paradise: Poetry of Papua New Guinea*, edited by Ulli Beier, 1972. **Thomas Nelson and Sons Ltd:** *"Sparrowhawk,"* originally titled "Falcon of the Heights," and *"Threshing Song,"* originally titled "First Song" from "The Threshing Songs of Angasmayo," reprinted from *The Singing Mountaineers: Songs and Tales of the Quechua People*, collected by Jose Maria Arguedas and edited by Ruth Tephan, 1957. **Anderson, Wanni Wibulswasdi 1973:** *"Crocodile! Crocodile!"* excerpt reprinted from dissertation (folklore and folklife) titled *Children's Play and Games in Rural Thailand; A Study in Enculturation and Socialisation*. **University of Texas at Austin:** *"I'll Return Again,"* excerpt reprinted from dissertation (anthropology) titled *Caribbean Folk Songs and Caribbean Culture* by Richard Eugene Hadel, 1972. **G. M. Bowra:** *"The Ant Workers,"* *"Lullaby"* and *"Star Song,"* excerpts from *Primitive Song*, printed by The Shenval Press, 1962. **Campbell, Carol Ann Arneson, Ph.D. 1983, University of Washington:** *"Coconut Song,"* excerpt from *Nyimbo Za Kiswahli: A Socio-Ethnomusicological Study of a Swahili Poetic Form*. Reprinted courtesy of **Ray Fadden, Akwesasne Six Nations Indian Museum, Onchiota, New York:** *"Song of the Sky Loom,"* originally titled "Indian Prayer." Reprinted courtesy of **Lloyd Carl Owle, P.O. Box 331, Cherokee, North Carolina 28719, U.S.A.:** *"The Rock,"* reprinted courtesy of **E. P. Dutton & Co.:** *"Voices That Beautify the Earth,"* from *Dawn Boy*.

The publishers have made every effort to contact holders of copyright material. If you have not received our correspondence, please contact us for inclusion in future editions.